<u>Time Management:</u>

Skills to Increase Productivity,

Become Organized, and Get

Things Done

Table Of Contents

Introduction

The clock is ticking and, once again, you are beyond behind in your work. You have been working diligently, or about as diligently as possible, and you still find yourself behind. This is a common occurrence in the world today; both in professional and personal settings. In most cases, the problem is not lack of time to do what is needed; it is lack of proper time management. Learning how to better manage your time can make all the difference in the world.

Time management is the practice of scheduling certain tasks that need to be done in a manner in which will optimize productivity. In this book we will cover: the different ways to better manage time, how to fight procrastination, and different boredom buster techniques that will not only optimize productivity, but also reduce stress. For many who have a lot to complete in a short amount of time, stress can be a contributing factor for not getting something finished.

Stress can be just as crippling as poor time management.

There are various ways to combat poor time management and still feel relaxed at the end of the day. This book is going to show you the way to be a more centered and productive person.

Chapter I: Writing is Your New Best Friend

The first question that you should ask yourself is: what do you want to get accomplished? Better time management does not necessarily just apply to getting your projects at work turned in on time. Learning to manage your time better can and should spill over into your personal life as well. Do you have a weight loss goal that you just haven't been able to hit yet? Is that bookshelf that you bought lying still not assembled in the corner? Is your life, on average, just in generally functional disarray?

In many instances, most people do not even realize how many unfinished things they have lying around. Poor time management affects our daily lives as much as it affects our professional ones. So, if you are going to get your professional life in shape, the best thing is to start at home. That's where writing comes in.

Writing is going to become your new best friend. Like in the days before technology was available for every fingertip, people used to write what they wanted to do. Though it is tempting to store all of your ideas in your phone, which is always within reach, it can also be a major form of distraction. How many times have you gone to go check your calendar, only to be quickly distracted by an app or a text? It happens more often than people think. Therefore, we are going to be going old school for this trick.

Find a Note Pad

When you have a designated area for something, it becomes easier to find that item because it has a home. This of this new note pad as your new home for your schedule. If you are a person who is always on the go, buy a note pad that is pocket sized. You do not necessarily have to get the note pads that are actual planners. How many of those do you have floating around our house? Probably quite a few. That's not to say that those do not work; it's just easy to start with something small that doesn't scream: Look, I'm planning!

A plain jane, normal note pad will work at first. Leave the more expensive, flashy ones for once you have actually gotten into the habit of keeping schedule. Once you do, you can get a formal planner as a reward (something we're going to cover later). Until then, you can use the planner to schedule different things to do during the day. A lot of people have said that writing down what they need to do during the day is actually very helpful in helping them remember the different tasks. After all, this practice has been around for longer than anyone can remember; why not use it to your advantage?

To Do List It Up

Now that you have your note pad, it is time to start making To Do lists. Yes, that's right; To Do lists. The archaic form of keeping track of your life that you thought died out with the 1950's supermom as well. Nope; these tricky little devils might be the most useful thing you have in your arsenal. The Ultimate Housewives definitely knew what they were doing when they used these.

A To Do list is comprised of everything that you need to get done during the day. The trick to an effective To Do list is not just to start jotting down things that need to get done, but rather to give them some sort of order. If you are a person who has various time sensitive things to do during the day, then written down your task in order of what is most urgent versus what can wait a while. In spite of that, if you work in order of largest tasks done first to maximize energy distribution, then a chronological list of most taxing to least daunting should be used. The only person who can tell you what kind of list you are going to need is you. Only you know how you operate the best.

The best time to design your To Do list is the day before. Generally speaking, if you wait until the end of the day, the you will know of everything that needs to be done. Once you get your list done, then you can go to bed for the night. For some people, writing down everything they need to get done can be cathartic; it relaxes them because they know exactly what they have to do the next day. This can lead to a better night's rest and more energy to go about your day.

See, better time management is already helping improve your life; even your health too.

Priorities First

When you take a look at your To Do list, it is important to bear in mind to follow the order that you put it in. Only in rare cases should you deviate from the plan that you have set for yourself. Make sure you get your priorities done first. The most important thing, whether they be time sensitive or just more important than anything else, should be the things that you do first. Here is an example of what your prioritized To Do list should look like:

To Do List For:			
Task	**Description of Task**	**Estimated Time to Complete**	**Checkmark**
Most important task here:	Detailed outline of what needs to be done	How long do you think this will take?	Check it off as you go
Next Important Task:	...	...	✓
I.E.: Pick up new shoes for work	Grab some black shoes from shopping center	Thirty Minutes	✓
Least Important Task:	...	...	✓

That is just an example of what your To Do list should look like. Most people notice that once they write down everything that they have to do, their day looks less hectic. It helps to categorize the thoughts in your head. That way you do not focus on the menial tasks, ignoring the most important one. Now, you will not have to worry about missing that lunch with your mother-in-law or being late to pick up the package from the post office before it closes. With each event categorized, your day should go a lot smoother.

Now, it is okay to leave some things undone; as long as they are not important. In the event that you do have to leave something undone, that's where the To Do list making at the end of the day comes in. When you check over your list at the end of the day, write down the things that you didn't complete on the next day's list. Once again, you are going to categorize what is most important. If the events from the previous day are as pertinent as some of the items of your next list, then do not list them first. In spite of that, it's helpful if you mark which item you had to carry over. That way you do not have to worry about constantly putting them off. The sooner you get things done, the sooner those things will be off of your mind. A clear mind means less stress which means a healthier life overall.

Chapter II: It's The Little Things that Weigh the Most

If you look around your home, you might notice things that have yet to be done. There could be a vast array of little things that are stacking up. When those little things stack up on you, it tends to weigh on the conscious. As things stack up, you might notice that your stress level rises as well. Here are some tips to help you get through the small things in life. After all, those are the lesser thought of events that are truly important.

Emails Are Like Warzones

Does your email have over five hundred emails? If so, that could make finding things damn near impossible. One of the reasons why people are late to events or never complete the task that they are assigned is because they have misplaced them. In today's day and age, you would assume that it is easier to keep track of everything that you need to do. That is actually quite the opposite. With everyone and their brother emailing you about different promotions and different employers trying to poach you from your current boss, not to mention the amount of anonymous spam that somehow slips through that less than effective spam filter, it can be difficult to find what you need. Differentiating between the important emails and senseless subscription updates can be daunting in and of its self.

The most important thing to bear in mind when trying to clear your inbox is that you get new emails every day. That may seem like a no-brainer, but it is often easily forgotten. With emails coming in everyday, it is important to keep on top of your inbox, lest it get out of control. All it takes is a week of forgetting to check your email and, next thing you know, your inbox reads that you have nine hundred and ninety-nine plus emails.

To start off the filtration process, the easiest thing to do is set up filters. Most email websites, such as yahoo and Gmail, have filters that you can set so that all incoming mail can be sectioned off into folders. This will help your inbox from seeming like the endless pit to nowhere. Any new emails that you get will immediately get sanctioned off into the appropriate zones. This also allows you to sift through the emails that are important to you and the ones that are not; such as that subscription to NeoPets from when you were in middle school.

Once you have done that, next comes the tricky part: going through your inbox and deleting the unnecessary. The filters do not immediately take all the emails that you have in your inbox and section it off. No, that would be to easy. In spite of that, they are useful, so do not skip that part. Now it is time to set some goals for yourself. This is another way that the ever-useful to-so list comes in handy.

Set a time during the day that you can go through and delete some unnecessary emails. If you are one of those people that has free time in the morning, then set the time for filtering then. It is not really recommended, since deleting emails can be tedious and frustrated. In spite of that, the important thing is to make sure that you get it done. It will only stack up if you do not.

Now, if you have more free time at night, which is a preferable time, then do so then. You can make it part of your nightly routine. Before you sit down to make your To Do list, go through your inbox and delete some of the junk in it. It does not really matter when you get it done, just as long as you do.

Another important thing to do is set a goal of how many emails you want to get deleted in a day. Is two thousand too daunting a task? Then make it smaller. As long as you delete over one hundred in a day, then your inbox will get steadily cleaner. In spite of that, bear in mind that the more you do per day, the faster you will be done. If you find it exhausting to go through and delete emails on a daily basis, and most people do, then set a higher goal. Just remember to stick to it.

Also, as you are going through your email, unsubscribe from needless emailers. This part is what can make the whole process harrowing, but the important thing to keep in mind is that you will not have to deal with that type of email anymore if you unsubscribe. If you still continue to get emails from the people that you have unsubscribed from, then message the site. Often times, if you voice a complaint then things tend to get resolved faster. After all, they want you to come back some day; possibly even recommend them to your friends.

In the end, if you limit the amount of clutter in your inbox, then you will be able to keep better track of the things in your life. If you are the type of person who works online and relies on your email to get your project and/or work, then this tip could be really helpful for you. Also, even if you are not the kind of person who relies on your email, sifting through it can help to alleviate some of the stress that you might be feeling. All in all, it is helpful to get that pesky inbox under control.

DIY's From Hell

Are you a do-it-yourselfer that is behind in your projects? Do you have half done projects lying around the house, just waiting to get your much needed attention? These projects, though they may seem unimportant when more pressing matters arise, can be part of the reason why you are stressing. Whether it be the numerous knitting projects that you started and just never finished or that nightstand that you bought and just never assembled, these unfinished projects lead to clutter. It has been reasoned that one component of stress is an overabundance of clutter. Help eliminate the clutter in both your home and your mind.

First thing to do is set aside time in your To Do list to go through all of your projects. Evaluate the reason why you dropped the project to begin with. Was it because you had something more important come up? Did you run out of material to complete it and just never came back to it? Either way, it is now time to figure out why these projects were ditched. Look around your home for the different things you just never finished and write a list. Keep that list someplace that it will not be lost amongst all the clutter. It is important that you make sure that you keep ahold of it; that way you can knock off things as you do them.

Once you've evaluated what you need for these projects, put it on your list to go pick them up. If you have everything that you need at your disposal, then you will not have an excuse for not finishing the projects. The sooner you pick up the necessary items the better. That way, you can start finishing projects and getting the items checked off your list faster. Remember, less clutter means less stress.

After you've gotten everything you need to complete your projects, it is time to set aside time to do them. Start with the large things. Set aside time during your less busy days, because every day is bound to be too busy to do trivial tasks, to complete a part of the project. Often times, once you get started, you might find yourself getting lost in the project and complete more than you said you would. Even in the event that you do not, you will at least have a goal to complete that will make the project get steadily more finished.

Once all the large projects have been finished, it is time to start on the smaller ones. Set aside time each day to complete one or more small projects. The more you complete, the closer you will be to being finished.

You will begin to see the clutter in your life shrink until it is basically nothing. This will make things easier to find around your home.

Now, for future projects, set a goal for when you want them completed. If it is something small, sit down and refuse to get up until you have completed it; emergencies withstanding. Put any projects that you might decide to do on your To Do list. This will ensure that they get completed. Though you can transfer items from previous To Do lists to the next day's, it is not recommended that you do these for projects. This is especially important to bear in mind when you are trying to get projects accomplished. The longer you put them off, the more things will get stacked up.

Important Papers Scattered Like Leaves

Are you the kind of person who has important documents scattered in piles around your house? Do you have boxes upon boxes of receipts that are older than your current license? If that is the case, then this could be adding clutter to your house. It is important to get these under control so that you can eliminate the clutter in your home.

When it comes to important papers, you do not want to just get rid of them. A whole lot valuable information is enclosed in those piles of papers that you do not want just anyone to get their hands on. Bank account information, social security numbers, addresses, and your full name are all things that could be used against you by petty thieves. That is why it is important to dispose of these things properly. Being lazy with trashing important documents could lead to bigger headaches down the road. Why would you do that when the point of managing your time better is to lead to less stress, not more?

The first thing to do is get a shredder. Shredders, though some may be pretty costly, are a worthwhile investment. Especially is you have a lot of sensitive documents to dispose of. Once you've acquired a shredder, next start with small steps. Put aside time in your To Do list to get rid of a certain amount per day. It is just like with everything else; you have to start small and plug your way through until you finish. If you have everything sectioned off into boxes, then start with one box at a time. If you do not have any reason or rhyme to your collection of past bills and W-2s, then start with a chunk and aim to make a visible difference.

Remember, not everything is trash. Weed through what is important and scrap the rest. In spite of that, make sure to categorize the important documents. Make boxes, or even get a nifty filing cabinet, and label off sections that have cast amounts of paper. Have a bunch of random items lying around that do not have a home? Make a miscellaneous folder with a guide that has everything in the folder on it. This will help you stay more organized.

You might be asking: how can organizing old bills help me manage time better? Well, have you ever spent hours searching for something that you need, but just can't find because of the amount of clutter that you have? If you organize it all, then you will not have to worry about doing that ever again. De-cluttering is just as important in managing your time as it helps you in the long run.

Cleaning House

Another helpful way to help manage your time is by keeping your home clean. Cleaning house can help minimize the amount of time spent looking for things. Searching through the junk can be hard if there's a lot of it. Cleaning up can help to eliminate the problems that might arise in the future. Learning how to manage your time better is all about thinking ahead. By setting aside time to clean different parts of the house, you will find that you have more time to spend doing the things you want in the long run.

Go back to your handy dandy To Do list. Amongst the various events that you have for the day, make sure to log a different part of the house to clean every day. By putting it in your list, you can make sure that these things get done. Make sure to keep in mind that cleaning should never be put off for the next day. That's how you got into the mess that you are currently in, isn't it? And yes, the pun was intended.

Prioritize which parts of the house need cleaned on a daily basis and which just need to be cleaned sporadically. The kitchen? That's an everyday task. You cook every day, in most instances, so there will always be a mess to clean in there. The living room? Unless you live with children or a large amount of people, the living room should only need a touching up at the end of the day. This tip is only valid after you have cleaned the living room.

The best thing to do is set aside a day to do a deep clean. Whip out the cleaning rags and the cleaner and just go to town. Make this your cleaning conquer day. You could even do this as often as once a month to ensure that everything will be clean on a consist basis. Been meaning to get to that dust that has collected on the ceiling fans? Do it on the deep clean day.

You will notice that as you clean, the air in your home will get clearer. After a few days, you begin to wonder why you hadn't done this sooner. In spite of that, you want to avoid the slump that comes with the nature of being human. You do not want to lax on the cleaning or it will stack up. That is why you clean a little bit every day. Doing this will ensure that if you have a surprise visitor come over, you will not have to rush around like a mad person cleaning. In the long run, you will experience less stress and even less allergies, since these are born out of dust that is hiding around your home. Do this and you will not have to worry a whole lot.

Chapter III: Self-Evaluate Like a Boss

Now that you've figured out what different projects you have lying around and how to make a To Do list, it is time to introspect. That is right; no time management plan would be complete with a little self-evaluation. Take look at everything that you do on a daily basis. Are you the kind of person who can spend hours watch television or on social media? You might think of it as a relaxation technique, but you are actually just procrastinating. You are putting things off for a later date in favor of doing something that requires very little brain power. If you want to manage your time better and get more things done during the day, then you have to stop the bad habits you have built

Take Stock

Look at everything you do in an ordinary. How are you spending your time? Do you run around like a chicken with your head off with never enough time to do everything? Just know that it doesn't have to be like that. Look at everything that you are doing during the day. Think about all the times where you sit there doing something less than productive. A whole lot time could be saved if you cut those things out. Now, that does not mean that you have to stop having fun. What kind of life would you be living if you didn't have fun on a regular basis? Not a fun one, that's for certain.

Do you spend a lot of time in the morning picking out your clothes for the day? That time that you spent trying on perfectly good outfit after perfectly good outfit could be better spent doing something else. Pick out your clothes before you go to bed at night. Chances are, you will be too tired after a day of work and everything else you have to do to try on a million different options. That and you will be more focused on what your day is going to look like the next day, that way you can pick accordingly.

Do you live in a place with weather that turns at the drop of a hat? Check the weather report for the next day and plan accordingly. Take a look at your to-so list and figure out what you are going to be doing during the day. Are you spending a day in the office and then going out after? Choose an outfit that can easily convert from day to nightlife; that way you do not have to rush home after work to change. Doing this can cut down on the amount of time you spend doing senselessly time consuming things.

When taking stock, do not berate yourself for what you are doing. Do not tear yourself down for spending hours catching up on the latest episodes of your new favorite. Instead, multi-task that time. Remember the projects that you have lying around? Pick up one of those and work on it while you watch television. Not only will you feel better for getting some accomplished while having some down time, but you will also get to do the things that you want to do without the guilt that usually follows.

The Important Things in Life

While you are self-evaluating, make sure to prioritize here. What brings you the most joy in the way you spend your free time? If checking your social media makes you happy, then do so while cleaning or sifting through some of the piles of important documents. That way you can maximize the way you spend your time. Your free time is precious. However, if you have too much of it, it can actually be more harmful than helpful. You might be resistant to changing what you do in your free time. After all, it is a time when you can do something that you thoroughly enjoy.

In spite of that, if something in your free time excursions is actually stressing you out, then cut it out. It might be hard to see what might be stressing you, but pay close attention. Think about how you feel after you do certain, unnecessary tasks. Do you feel happy? Do you actually feel more dragged down than uplifted? If the feeling you get is the latter than stop doing that to yourself. If may seem important to keep updated on every little thing in your friends' life, but that isn't the case; not if it is costing you your sanity. Small things like that, that cause you stress, are not worth doing to yourself. Stress wears on the body. By adding unneeded stress to your body, you are actually physically harming yourself. Though this has become a socially acceptable form of self-harm, you do not have to accept it. Strive to do better for your body; it is the only one you have got.

The best way to figure out if you can live without doing something is to try it. Purge yourself of social media, or something of the like, for a few days. During this time, you might jones for the media outlet that you've let go. It is only natural for this to occur. Some people have noted that social media is as much an addiction as any of the drugs out there. In spite of that, you have to show discipline. If you see, at the end of it all, that you do not need it as much as you thought, then you might want to seriously think about reintroducing the outlet into your life. On the other hand, if you find that your life is made harder by not having that outlet in your life, then please do continue with that trend. In the end, you will learn if something is truly important to you.

Creative Input

Once you've evaluated what is harming your time management, fix it. It is just that simple. If you know something is bad for the way you spend your time, then stop doing it. It may take some time and effort to perfect it, but it is well worth it. Too many people, in this day and age, waste time that they could be using more fruitfully. Wasting time is what got you into reading this book to begin with. If you were not wasting time, you would have better time management. Now, that is not to say that everything that you do is a waste of time. Everything is fine in moderation. The key is to find he balance between good and bad, as opposed to just bad.

Instead, try putting that time to good use. Whether it is finding a way to relax or getting some more work done; just find a way to use that time more effectively. You would be surprised how much time you have if you cut out all the bad routines you have. You see this practice in your everyday life. Think of all the gardeners, doctors, and artists out there. They all share a common trait. If they find something to be detrimental to the overall outcome, then they get rid of it. In order for new growth to happen, you have to cut away the dead stuff. Think of time wasting activities as dead stuff. Prune back the deceased, useless exercises that you have in your life to make way for a new and better you. You will be surprised how you feel in the end.

Chapter IV: Work Smarter, Not Harder

For a few of you, you were probably wondering when we might get to the professional side of time management. Well, before you serve the dinner, you have to cook it right? The same analogy fits in to this exercise, as do most things in life. Before you take care of what makes your world go around, you have to take care of your world first. That being said, the work aspect of life is also important. It is often a hassle to balance all the balls that life throws at you. In spite of that, if you learn to manage your time better, then you will find that your work day will go smoother. Let's get started:

Prioritize, Prioritize, Prioritize

Like in all things in life, you have to prioritize at work as well. Has your boss been harping on you to complete that important project that is way overdue? You keep trying to make time for it, but often find ways to distract yourself? Relax; it happens to the best of us. Nevertheless, it is important to complete important projects in a timely manner. If you make a pattern of late work, then consequences will come. This applies even if you work for yourself. In the real world, everyone has someone to answer to.

The best thing to do is to sit down and evaluate what needs to be done. Make yet another list, they are more important than one might think, to keep track of everything that needs to get done. Once you've figured out what you need to do, you can sort it into an order that signifies which is more important and which is less so. By doing this, you free up your head for the important stuff: figuring out how to get everything accomplished.

Does your list seem to go on and on forever? That's what the system of putting things into order comes in handy. Make sure to complete the most important and time sensitive things first. By doing this, you will find yourself more stress free than if you just run around trying to complete everything you have to do. Also, remember to stay relaxed. The more agitated you get, the less likely you are to get everything done. Remaining relaxed, in the mindset that you will accomplish everything needed, will keep you from getting too in over your head.

As the days go by, knock more and more things off your list. You will notice that, as the list gets shorter, you will become more relaxed. Just try to remember to breathe and focus on one task at a time. After all, you are only human and making mistakes is in our nature. Do not focus on what you did to get in the situation that you are in. Instead, focus on how you will feel once you are out of it. This an apply to all aspects of life, but you are focusing on work at the moment. That is another important point, but we will get to that later.

Delegating Exists For A Reason

If you are in the position to delegate, utilize it! Most people prefer to get their tasks done by themselves. If we have our hands on something, it can't go wrong, right? Well, that mindset leads to more stress than is necessary. If you can delegate some of the tasks that are plaguing you at work, then it is best to do so. That is what help is there to do; help!

This is especially true if you work for yourself. If you are self-employed then you probably have people working for you. If you do not, then it might be a good idea to get some employees. Utilize the people working for you. You are not paying them to sit around and do nothing. You might not want to come off as a demanding boss; one who's always asking way more of their employees than is possible. In spite of that, taking all the tasks on yourself might have an adverse reaction as well. It might make your employees think that you do not value them. You do not want that to happen. Instead, use them for what you pay them for.

Take the initiative to get as much work done in a day as is possible. Once again, that means rely on the people that work for you. Now, if you think that something still will not get done, then keep track of things. Monitor, without stalking, who has which project. Keep on top of things, so that you know if things are being completed. This is a system that works in all of the major businesses around the world. Just make sure not to harass your employees. If something is so important that you feel the need to check on it every few minutes, then do that task yourself. Not everything is for delegating, but it is also not all for you to do.

Delegating also works even if you do not work for yourself? Do you work in a setting where there are multiple people working on this project too? Use this to your advantage. Make sure that everyone is pulling their weight on the project. It is not your sole responsibility to get everything done when a whole group is working on something. Is someone in your group refusing to pull their share of the work? Do not stand for it. Try and talk to this person; reason with them that, when they do not do their work, it puts more stress on you. If this does not work, then tell your supervisor. You should not feel like a tattle-tell; that is what supervisors are there for. You should not stress yourself out so that someone else can shirk off their responsibilities.

In the end, delegating could help you free up your time to complete some of the work that is piling up on your desk. Just make sure not to hover over who you turned the reins over to. If you are going to hand something off to someone else, make sure it is something that you can afford to do. And remember, the name of the time managing game is to help you relax.

A Focused Mind Makes an Empty Desk

Getting distracted is a normal occurrence for all people. Do not tear yourself down for getting distracted in either frivolous activities or the little things that need to get done. Instead, try harder to make yourself more focused. Do not let distractions plague your mind and you will find yourself being more productive than ever.

To help cut out distraction, concentrate on what mainly distracts you. Are you the type of person who like to do little things when they're feeling stressed out by the bigger picture? While this is helpful, it is also important not to get too distracted by these things. If you let your mind focus on those things, you will never finish the bigger project. This will only further delay the evitable which is not getting anything of import done.

To cut down on getting distracted, make sure that you have everything that you could possibly need before you sit down to work. Grab that cup of coffee or tea, sharpen al pencils, grab any electronic charger that you might need, set your playlist, and just work. By getting everything that you might need, you cut down on the amount of times that you might need to get up. By having all your needs around you, you can focus all your concentration on what you are doing and not when that pot of coffee in the breakroom might be done.

Now that you have eliminated anything that you might need, focus. Sit down and start working. Only allow yourself to get up for bathroom breaks and emergencies only. If your boss is calling you into his office, you obviously cannot ignore that. In spite of that, anything short of the building burning down, someone dying and you can help them, or potentially getting fired shouldn't pull you from your seat. Just remember, if it is not important, then it can wait until later. Your main focus, at the moment, is productivity.

Optimize the Work Space

One of the most important things that you can do to have better time management at work is to organize your work area. You might notice that, if your work space is in disarray, then it will be harder to get things accomplished. You do not know where anything is and that causes delays. It is those delays that, inevitably, lead to wasting time. If you organize your work space, the you optimize productivity in it.

Start by sorting through the, undoubtedly, endless piles of papers that you have. Papers, for some odd reason, like to accumulate in groups. They are almost like sheep, in that respect. If you sort through these, getting rid of those that you do not need, then you do not have to worry about losing the important documents you have lying around. You will know where all your reports are at the exact moment that you need them.

Next, create a home for everything. Create a filing system, like you did at home, you better keep track of things. Then, make sure to adhere to it. Otherwise, you wasted all that time doing absolutely nothing. It is important to keep on top of your sorting system. The moment you let it slack is the moment that you start losing track of things.

By the time you are done optimizing, everything should have a home it can call its own. By doing these simple things, you will not have to worry about getting behind in your work. Not only is it helpful for keeping you organized, but it also will help you feel more at peace. When you declutter your workspace, you open up the environment. This, surprisingly, allows for thoughts to flow easier.

Chapter V: Create a Rewards System

Contrary to popular belief, working on yourself does not have to be all work. In fact, it important to create a reward system. By doing this, it makes the thought of working on yourself less daunting. Everything in life is easier when you have something to look forward to. It is those small things that can make the somewhat daunting tasks seems less so.

Identify Your Bliss

What do you do for fun? Do you like to do crosswords or go biking? Whatever your passion is, find it. By taking the time to do this, you open up a reward portal. The important thing to remember is this task should be relaxing. If you enjoy doing, such as playing video games, but do not really relax at it, then this will not help. Find something that relaxes you.

If you do not currently do anything that helps you relax, try looking up some things on the internet. The internet is full of useful tips for relaxing. Put in your

To Do list a certain amount of time during the day to find something that helps you relax. Some people prefer to take a bubble bath. Others like to bake or go for a walk. There are even some relaxation techniques that a bit more eccentric. What your relaxation technique might be, use it. Do not worry about how you might look to others doing it. If your ultimate form of relaxation comes from cuddling up with a blanket and a teddy bear, then grab blankie and Mr. Snuggles. Whatever it may be, just make sure to make it your own and as relaxing as possible.

Time to Relax

On especially busy days, it might seem like the day goes on forever. This is where your reward system comes into play. Work in certain times during the day that you can relax. This will keep you from getting too overwhelmed in the middle of the day. If you get overwhelmed, then you get less done. One again, it is important to remember to stay calm and relaxed. That is why you exercise your reward. That way you can keep a level head throughout the day.

Another important thing to do is to make sure that you put aside time each day to relax. Yes, this is important to do on busy days, but people do not only get stressed out on busy days. At the end of each day, take some time to relax. This is all a part of the reward system. If you focus on the reward you have coming at the end of the day, then it makes it easier to get through the day. Not every day is going to be hectic; some might just drag on forever. Choose times like these to focus on the reward at the end of the day.

Another useful way to use the reward system is to reward yourself after daunting task. Did you finally complete that bookshelf that's been sitting in the corner; the one from Chapter Two? Then reward yourself. It is important to reward the major accomplishments you have made. Now, if losing weight was a goal that you accomplished, then do not choose something like eating an entire cake as a reward. Make the rewards fit the task accomplished.

It Is There for A Reason

The last thing to bear in mind, in regards to the reward system, is to make sure that you use it. Make time for each reward to happen. Plan it into your day if you have a hectic one. Just make sure that you do this. Otherwise, your days will begin to blur together. That would make the To Do list seem like more of a chore than it has to be.

On the other hand, it is important not to overuse the reward system. Do not reward yourself for minor things, unless it is on a very rare occasion. This is just another way to waste time. It isn't advised to reward yourself when nothing was truly accomplished. Instead, do a whole slew of smaller tasks and then reward yourself. At the end of the day, you want to reward yourself for completing something that was very hard or took a lot of time. Just make sure to use it for the right reasons.

Chapter VI: Build It Better Than Before

One of the crucial aspects of better time management is building a routine out of the tips that you have learned. It is important to incorporate these things into your everyday life. We have touched on this subject before, but it is one that requires further explanation. Making better time management a part of your daily routine is important. It makes the little steps that you take to improve your life seem less harrowing. Every person has a set routine. You might not think that you do, but it is there; hidden below the slew of things you have to get done every day. Take a second to determine what your routine is and how it is hurting you in the long run. Now, find ways to make it more helpful.

Buckle Down

The key to building routine out of managing your time better is to exercise some discipline. If you can, make it like a New Year's resolution. No, not like that resolution from almost a decade ago about how you would go for a walk every day. Instead, buckle down and get it done. It takes six weeks to build a habit and that is what you want this to be, a habit. If you make it a habit, then it makes it less of a chore.

Some ways that you can easily incorporate these tips into your life is to switch a few things around. If you are the kind of person who likes to have coffee in the morning while you read the paper, then simply switch the newspaper for your To Do list. Make it a routine. It is going to take some conscious effort, but the payoff will be amazing. Use that time in the morning to go over everything that you put on your list the night before. This will not only be more helpful in starting your day than simply catching up on the news of the world, but it will also start your day with a sense of ease. The ease comes from knowing exactly what you have to do and know that you have enough time to do it. This knowledge can actually be very calming.

If you are the type of person who can not back down from a challenge, then challenge yourself. Make a mantra of it. Constantly remind yourself that you have a list and you got to stick to it. By keeping these tips fresh in your mind, you are less likely to stray from the beaten path. Just try to remember: you are doing this to make your life easier. You do not want to rush around every single day like the sky is falling. That is the perfect way to miss the little treasures that life has hidden for you. The only thing you have to do is stop and look for them. However, you cannot do that if you are rushing from one place to the other. So, build a routine around making your life easier.

Show some fortitude in your list making. If you have a hard time keeping track of things, make sure that your list is in a place that you will easily see it each morning. Make the conscious effort to place the list there every night. It might even be helpful to open your note pad to the next day's list; that way you cannot easily miss it.

Make It Shine

Another helpful way to not forget your list is to make it stand out. Color the pages and/or the entire note pad. Use bright, eye catching colors that will make it hard to miss. The most important part of making a list part of your routine is to remember to do it. So, take the time to make your lists hard to miss.

It is time to break out the glitter pens and highlighting markers. Jazz up each page at the end of the day as you make your list. Are you good a drawing? Even if you aren't, draw some of the things you have to do the next day on the page. There is a reason why there are so many new adult coloring books. Someone somewhere realized the pure, unadulterated joy that can come with coloring things. So, put that to good use. Do you have to take the dog to the vet? Draw an adorable puppy on the side of the page with a bandage on his paw. You do not have to treat it like a masterpiece, just get it colorful. However, if it will help you remember, treat each page like it is a work of art.

Also, once you have gotten in the habit of keeping a regular note pad, buy one that is atheistically pleasing. If you like rainbows, then hit up the children school supply section and find one with rainbows on it. Whatever suits your fancy, do it. Do not worry about what other people might think. If you get strange looks on the subway for being a grown individual with a puppies note pad, just laugh it off. They do not know that you are striving to be a better you. Plus, what are the chances that you are going to see them again? The opinions of others should have very little say in what you choose to do with your life.

Make It a Family Thing

If you live in a large household, you might notice that your routine intersects with other people's. If you live with your family, this can hinder you in some ways, On the other hand, it does not have to be that way. Get the whole family in on managing their time better. If you stop and look around you, you might notice that everyone else is exercising poor time management as well. This is a problem that hardly ever focuses on just one person. So get the whole gang in on it.

Set the children down and have them tell you their schedule. Work it into your To Do list. Explain to them how some changes are going to happen. If you do not explain things to them, they might not understand why you are acting differently. Sure, people are resistant to change. Conversely, they are more resistant to change when they do not know that it is happening. So, let the people in your life in on the changes. Not only will it help them, but it will also help make you more accountable for the changes that you are making in your life too.

Make To Do lists a part of the family routine. Get a dry erase or chalk board for the kitchen. You can attach magnets, or get one of those newfangled ones that comes with the magnets already attached, and put it on the refrigerator. They can add what they need to do as well as help you keep track of what everyone is doing during the week. This knowledge will bring you piece of mind. Just remember to conquer everything on a day to day basis.

If you live alone, call up a family member to help you in this journey. When you have an accountability partner, it makes it easier for you not to slack off. Call a sibling, parent, or close extended family member. You can both resolve to exercise better time management. Then, you can both make sure that the other person is doing what they need to do. If you are the type of person who thrives on competition, then make better time management a challenge against the other person. Set up a group reward system and shame system that can be exercised upon succeeding a failing. With more than one person working at a goal, that goal is usually easier to achieve. You see this practice all around you. You would not have one construction worker building a skyscraper, would you? No, you would have a team. If you are a team player, then build a team. Figure out a way to manage time better that works better for you.

Chapter VII: Stick to It

Now that you have found ways to maximize your time, it is imperative that you stick to it. It may seem tasking at first, but as long as you stick with it, it will become like second nature. There are tons of people out there that use these tips and it make their lives a whole lot easier. If you have ever seen a person who just always seems to know what they are doing and where they are going in life, it is probably because they have planned accordingly. No one is just born, inherently knowing how to manage their time properly.

Start Small

Start with small task. You do not want to overwhelm yourself before you even make any progress. Start with just a list. Make it a list of things you want to get done during the day. Then build on that list. Start marking off ways that you can enhance you time. Start tacking on different tips that you learned in this book that will help make your life easier. Before you know it, you will be more organized and using your time more efficiently.

If you find that you are stuck in a rut with starting small, then branch out. Try something else. The most important thing to keep in mind is that this is your life. Not all advice works for all people. Find something that works for you. Is writing down what you are going to do only stressing you out more? Than do not do it. The simple thing to bear in mind is that if it does not work for you, then you should not be doing it. Do not force yourself into a mold that does not fit. Instead, find something that will.

Know When Enough Is Enough

You have to know when you are in over your head. If you look around you and all you see is clutter, then it is definitely time for an overhaul. Starting small does help, but not when there is a lot to do. In these instances, you only find yourself becoming more and more frustrated by your current life status. If this is the case for you, then it is time for a drastic change.

Make a day out of cleaning up your life. It is going to take a lot of effort, but it will definitely be worth it in the end. Use the reward system to help you get through it. Set milestones of things that you want completed. After each milestone, reward yourself in a small way that will help you stay focused and keep you from giving up. This will help get everything done that you need to get done.

Once you have completed everything you need to in your overhaul, it is time for the big reward. If you like wine, pour yourself a glass and look over all the progress you have made. Just make sure that there is actual progress. Stay focused and push through it. In the end, the results will be even better than the reward.

A Promise to Yourself

The whole point of better time management is to make your life easier. Therefore, do not do it for anyone other than yourself. If you do it because people recommend it, then it will seem like more of a hassle than anything. You have to be the one that wants to change. If, in the end, you find that you liked things better the way they were, then revert. However, do not start managing your time better because of what the world says.

This is where you make a promise to yourself. Promise yourself that you are going to become that person that you see and wonder how they do it all. If you promise yourself, you are less likely to let yourself down. Do not become lazy with your commitment. It is all about being a better you, so better yourself by being more active in your life. This is a change that you wanted to make so see it through. Otherwise, all your To Do lists are going to end up like the bookcase that never got finished. They will simply lay in a corner, completely forgotten. You do not want that. You want to come out on top. After all, the view from the top is always the best.

Conclusion

Now that you have all these tips in mind, it is time to start acting. Do not simply put it off for a later date. The best time to start is right now. If you put it off, it will be forgotten. So, grab a random note pad and start making lists immediately. You will be taken back by how good it will feel to finally be a bit more organized.

Keep in mind that you are going to struggle. There are going to be times when you do not necessarily feel like doing what is on your To Do list. That is perfectly fine. Just make sure that you do not make it a habit. If you find yourself exhausted with making lists and checking them twice, then take a relaxation day. Just spend the day lounging around in your pajamas. The list will be there tomorrow. Just remember to pick it back up the next day.

If you stick to the tips and work hard at it, your life will become seamlessly organized. You will find yourself stressing less and enjoying life more. Eventually, you will not even need a note pad to keep track of things. Making To Do lists will be so commonplace for you, that you will be doing it in your sleep. Make it a part of your everyday life and just see how much your life improves.